The Collected Poems of
Lord Alfred Douglas

AMS PRESS
NEW YORK

Photo by W. Ransford, London, N.W.

Alfred Bruce Douglas

The Collected Poems of
Lord Alfred Douglas

London
Martin Secker
xvii Buckingham Street
Adelphi

Library of Congress Cataloging in Publication Data

Douglas, Alfred Bruce, Lord, 1870-1945.
   The collected poems of Lord Alfred Douglas.

   Reprint of the 1919 ed. published by M. Secker,
London.
   I. Title.
PR6007.086A6   1976   821'.9'12   75-41079
ISBN 0-404-14659-7

Reprinted from the edition of 1919, London
First AMS edition published in 1976
Manufactured in the United States of America

AMS PRESS INC.
NEW YORK, N.Y.

TO MY MOTHER

THE poems in this collection, dating from about 1890 to the present year 1919, are printed in something approximating to chronological order. Consequently readers are invited to note that the best poems are not, generally speaking, to be found in the beginning of the volume.   A. D.

Contents

9

Apologia

Tell me not of Philosophies,
   Of morals, ethics, laws of life ;*
Give me no subtle theories,
   No instruments of wordy strife.
I will not forge laborious chains
   Link after link, till seven times seven,
I need no ponderous iron cranes
   To haul my soul from earth to heaven.
But with a burnished wing,
   Rainbow-hued in the sun,
   I will dive and leap and run
In the air, and I will bring
Back to the earth a heavenly thing,
   I will dance through the stars
   And pass the blue bars
Of heaven. I will catch hands with God
   And speak with Him,
   I will kiss the lips of the seraphim
   And the deep-eyed cherubim ;
I will pluck of the flowers that nod
   Row upon row upon row,
In the infinite gardens of God,

* For the author's present view of these and similar sentiments in his early
poems, see " Note " page 125.

To the breath of the wind of the sweep of the lyres,
    And the cry of the strings
    And the golden wires,
    And the mystical musical things
That the world may not know.

Oxford, 1892.

Autumn Days

I have been through the woods to-day
    And the leaves were falling,
Summer had crept away,
    And the birds were not calling.

And the bracken was like yellow gold
    That comes too late,
When the heart is sad and old,
    And death at the gate.

Ah, mournful Autumn ! Sad,
    Slow death that comes at last,
I am mad for a yesterday, mad !
    I am sick for a year that is past !

Though the sun be like blood in the sky
    He is cold as the lips of hate,
And he fires the sere leaves as they lie
    On their bed of earth, too late.

They are dead, and the bare trees weep
    Not loud as a mortal weeping,
But as sorrow that sighs in sleep,
    And as grief that is still in sleeping.

The Hut, 1890.

To Shakespeare

Most tuneful singer, lover tenderest,
Most sad, most piteous, and most musical,
Thine is the shrine more pilgrim-worn than all
The shrines of singers ; high above the rest
Thy trumpet sounds most loud, most manifest.
Yet better were it if a lonely call
Of woodland birds, a song, a madrigal,
Were all the jetsam of thy sea's unrest.

For now thy praises have become too loud
On vulgar lips, and every yelping cur
Yaps thee a pæan ; the whiles little men,
Not tall enough to worship in a crowd,
Spit their small wits at thee. Ah ! better then
The broken shrine, the lonely worshipper.

Amoris Vincula

As a white dove that, in a cage of gold,
   Is prisoned from the air, and yet more bound
By love than bars, and will not wings unfold
   To fly away, though every gate be found
Unlocked and open ; so my heart was caught,
   And linked to thine with triple links of love.
But soon, a dove grown wanton, false it sought
   To break its chain, and faithless quite to rove
Where thou wouldst not ; and with a painted bird
   Fluttered far off. But when a moon was past,
Grown sick with longing for a voice unheard
   And lips unkissed, spread wings and home flew fast.
And lo ! what seemed a sword to cleave its chain,
   Was but a link to rivet it again.

A Summer Storm

Alas ! how frail and weak a little boat
I have sailed in.   I called it Happiness,
And I had thought there was not storm nor stress
Of wind so masterful but it would float
Blithely in their despite ; but lo ! one note
Of harsh discord, one word of bitterness,
And a fierce overwhelming wilderness
Of angry waters chokes my gasping throat.

I am near drowned in this unhappy sea,
I will not strive, let me lie still and sink,
I have no joy to live.   Oh ! unkind love !
Why have you wounded me so bitterly ?
That am as easily wounded as a dove
Who has a silver throat and feet of pink.

A Winter Sunset

The frosty sky, like a furnace burning,
   The keen air, crisp and cold,
   And a sunset that splashes the clouds with gold ;
But my heart to summer turning.

Come back, sweet summer ! come back again !
   I hate the snow,
   And the icy winds that the north lands blow,
And the fall of the frozen rain.

I hate the iron ground,
   And the Christmas roses,
   And the sickly day that dies when it closes,
With never a song or a sound.

Come back ! come back ! with your passionate heat
   And glowing hazes,
   And your sun that shines as a lover gazes,
And your day with the tired feet.

In Summer

There were the black pine trees,
    And the sullen hills
    Frowning ; there were trills
    Of birds, and the sweet hot sun,
    And little rills
    Of water, everyone
Singing and prattling ; there were bees

Honey-laden, tuneful, a song
    Far-off, and a timid air
    That sighed and kissed my hair,
    My hair that the hot sun loves.
    The day was very fair,
    There was wooing of doves,
And the shadows were not yet long.

And I lay on the soft green grass,
    And the smell of the earth was sweet,
    And I dipped my feet
    In the little stream ;
    And was cool as a flower is cool in the heat,
    And the day lay still in a dream,
And the hours forgot to pass.

And you came, my love, so stealthily
    That I saw you not
    Till I felt that your arms were hot
    Round my neck, and my lips were wet
    With your lips, I had forgot
    How sweet you were.   And lo ! the sun has set,
And the pale moon came up silently.

Thuringewald, 1892.

In Winter

Oh ! for a day of burning noon
   And a sun like a glowing ember,
Oh ! for one hour of golden June,
   In the heart of this chill November.

I can scarcely remember the Spring's soft breath
   Or imagine the Summer hazes.
The yellow woods are so damp with death
   That I have forgotten the daisies.

Oh ! to lie watching the sky again,
   From a nest of hot grass and clover,
Till the stars come out like golden rain
   When the lazy day is over.

And crowning the night with an aureole,
   As the clouds kiss and drift asunder,
The moon floats up like a luminous soul,
   And the stars grow pale for wonder.

In Sarum Close

Tired of passion and the love that brings
Satiety's unrest, and failing sands
Of life, I thought to cool my burning hands
In this calm twilight of gray Gothic things :
But Love has laughed, and, spreading swifter wings
Than my poor pinions, once again with bands
Of silken strength my fainting heart commands,
And once again he plays on passionate strings.

But thou, my love, my flower, my jewel, set
In a fair setting, help me, or I die,
To bear Love's burden ; for that load to share
Is sweet and pleasant, but if lonely I
Must love unloved, 'tis pain ; shine we, my fair,
Two neighbour jewels in Love's coronet.

The Sphinx

I gaze across the Nile ; flamelike and red
The sun goes down, and all the western sky
Is drowned in sombre crimson ; wearily
A great bird flaps along with wings of lead,
Black on the rose-red river. Over my head
The sky is hard green bronze, beneath me lie
The sleeping ships ; there is no sound, or sigh
Of the wind's breath,—a stillness of the dead.

Over a palm tree's top I see the peaks
Of the tall pyramids ; and though my eyes
Are barred from it, I know that on the sand
Crouches a thing of stone that in some wise
Broods on my heart ; and from the darkening land
Creeps Fear and to my soul in whisper speaks.

British Agency, Cairo, 1893.

Impression de Nuit

See what a mass of gems the city wears
Upon her broad live bosom ! row on row
Rubies and emeralds and amethysts glow.
See ! that huge circle like a necklace, stares
With thousands of bold eyes to heaven, and dares
The golden stars to dim the lamps below,
And in the mirror of the mire I know
The moon has left her image unawares.

That's the great town at night : I see her breasts,
Pricked out with lamps they stand like huge black towers.
I think they move ! I hear her panting breath.
And that's her head where the tiara rests.
And in her brain, through lanes as dark as death,
Men creep like thoughts . . . The lamps are like pale
    flowers.

London, 1894.

To L—

Thou that wast once my loved and loving friend,
A friend no more, I had forgot thee quite,
Why hast thou come to trouble my delight
With memories ?   Oh ! I had clean made end
Of all that time, I had made haste to send
My soul into red places, and to light
A torch of pleasure to burn up my night.
What I have woven hast thou come to rend ?

In silent acres of forgetful flowers,
Crowned as of old with happy daffodils,
Long time my wounded soul has been a-straying,
Alas ! it has chanced now on sombre hours
Of hard remembrances and sad delaying,
Leaving green valleys for the bitter hills.

Night Coming Into a Garden

Roses red and white,
Every rose is hanging her head,
    Silently comes the lady Night,
    Only the flowers can hear her tread.

All day long the birds have been calling,
    Calling shrill and sweet,
They are still when she comes with her long robe falling,
    Falling down to her feet.

The thrush has sung to his mate,
    " She is coming ! hush ! she is coming ! "
She is lifting the latch at the gate,
    And the bees have ceased from their humming.

I cannot see her face as she passes
    Through my garden of white and red ;
But I know she has walked where the daisies and grasses
    Are curtseying after her tread.

She has passed me by with a rustle and sweep
    Of her robe (as she passed I heard it sweeping),
And all my red roses have fallen asleep,
    And all my white roses are sleeping.

Night Coming Out of a Garden

Through the still air of night
  Suddenly comes, alone and shrill,
Like the far-off voice of the distant light,
  The single piping trill
Of a bird that has caught the scent of the dawn,
  And knows that the night is over ;
(She has poured her dews on the velvet lawn
  And drenched the long grass and the clover),
And now with her naked white feet
  She is silently passing away,
  Out of the garden and into the street,
Over the long yellow fields of the wheat,
  Till she melts in the arms of the day.
And from the great gates of the East,
  With a clang and a brazen blare,
Forth from the rosy wine and the feast
  Comes the god with the flame-flaked hair ; ·
The hoofs of his horses ring
  On the golden stones, and the wheels
Of his chariot burn and sing,
  And the earth beneath him reels ;
And forth with a rush and a rout
  His myriad angels run,
And the world is awake with a shout,
  " He is coming ! The sun ! The sun ! "

Perkin Warbeck

i

At Turney in Flanders I was born
  Fore-doomed to splendour and sorrow,
For I was a king when they cut the corn,
  And they strangle me to-morrow.

ii

Oh ! why was I made so red and white,
  So fair and straight and tall ?
And why were my eyes so blue and bright,
  And my hands so white and small ?

iii

And why was my hair like the yellow silk,
  And curled like the hair of a king ?
And my body like the soft new milk
  That the maids bring from milking ?

iv

I was nothing but a weaver's son,
  I was born in a weaver's bed ;
My brothers toiled and my sisters spun,
  And my mother wove for our bread.

27

v

I was the latest child she had,
  And my mother loved me the best.
She would laugh for joy and anon be sad
  That I was not as the rest.

vi

For my brothers and sisters were black as the gate
  Whereby I shall pass to-morrow,
But I was white and delicate,
  And born to splendour and sorrow.

vii

And my father the weaver died full soon,
  But my mother lived for me ;
And I had silk doublets and satin shoon
  And was nurtured tenderly.

viii

And the good priests had much joy of me,
  For I had wisdom and wit ;
And there was no tongue or subtlety
  But I could master it.

ix

And when I was fourteen summers old
  There came an English knight,
With purple cloak and spurs of gold,
  And sword of chrysolite.

He rode through the town both sad and slow,
    And his hands lay in his lap ;
He wore a scarf as white as the snow,
    And a snow-white rose in his cap.

xi

And he passed me by in the market-place,
    And he reined his horse and stared,
And I looked him fair and full in the face,
    And he stayed with his head all bared.

xii

And he leaped down quick and bowed his knee,
    And took hold on my hand,
And he said, " Is it ghost or wraith that I see,
    Or the White Rose of England ? "

xiii

And I answered him in the Flemish tongue,
    " My name is Peter Warbeckke,
From Katherine de Faro I am sprung,
    And my father was John Osbeckke.

xiv

" My father toiled and weaved with his hand
    And bare neither sword nor shield
And the White Rose of fair England
    Turned red on Bosworth field."

xv

And he answered, " What matter for anything ?
    For God hath given to thee
The voice of the king and the face of the king,
    And the king thou shalt surely be."

xvi

And he wrought on me till the vesper bell,
    And I rode forth out of the town :
And I might not bid my mother farewell,
    Lest her love should seem more than a crown.

xvii

And the sun went down, and the night waxed black,
    And the wind sang wearily ;
And I thought on my mother, and would have gone back,
    But he would not suffer me.

xviii

And we rode, and we rode, was it nine days or three ?
    Till we heard the bells that ring
For " my cousin Margaret of Burgundy,"
    And I was indeed a king.

xix

For I had a hundred fighting men
    To come at my beck and call,
And I had silk and fine linen
    To line my bed withal.

xx

They dressed me all in silken dresses,
  And little I wot did they reck
Of the precious scents for my golden tresses,
  And the golden chains for my neck.

xxi

And all the path for " the rose " to walk
  Was strewn with flowers and posies,
I was the milk-white rose of York,
  The rose of all the roses.

xxii

And the Lady Margaret taught me well,
  Till I spake without lisping
Of Warwick and Clarence and Isabel,
  And " my father " Edward the King.

xxiii

And I sailed to Ireland and to France,
  And I sailed to fair Scotland,
And had much honour and pleasaunce,
  And Katherine Gordon's hand.

xxiv

And after that what brooks it to say
  Whither I went or why ?
I was as loath to leave my play
  And fight, as now to die.

xxv

For I was not made for wars and strife
    And blood and slaughtering,
I was but a boy that loved his life,
    And I had not the heart of a king.

xxvi

Oh ! why hath God dealt so hardly with me,
    That such a thing should be done,
That a boy should be born with a king's body
    And the heart of a weaver's son ?

xxvii

I was well pleased to be at the court,
    Lord of the thing that seems ;
It was merry to be a prince for sport,
    A king in a kingdom of dreams.

xxviii

But ever they said I must strive and fight
    To wrest away the crown,
So I came to England in the night
    And I warred on Exeter town.

xxix

And the King came up with a mighty host
    And what could I do but fly ?
I had three thousand men at the most,
    And I was most loath to die.

And they took me and brought me to London town,
  And I stood where all men might see ;
I, that had well-nigh worn a crown,
  In a shameful pillory !

And I cried these words in the English tongue,
  " I am Peter Warbeckke,
From Katherine de Faro I am sprung
  And my father was John Osbeckke.

" My father toiled and weaved with his hand,
  And bare neither sword nor shield ;
And the White Rose of fair England
  Turned red on Bosworth field."

And they gave me my life, but they held me fast
  Within this weary place ;
But I wrought on my guards ere a month was past,
  With my wit and my comely face.

And they were ready to set me free,
  But when it was almost done,
And I thought I should gain the narrow sea
  And look on the face of the sun,

xxxv

The lord of the tower had word of it,
    And, alas ! for my poor hope,
For this is the end of my face and my wit
    That to-morrow I die by the rope.

xxxvi

And the time draws nigh and the darkness closes,
    And the night is almost done.
What had I to do with their roses,
    I, the poor weaver's son ?

xxxvii

They promised me a bed so rich
    And a queen to be my bride,
And I have gotten a narrow ditch
    And a stake to pierce my side.

xxxviii

They promised me a kingly part
    And a crown my head to deck,
And I have gotten the hangman's cart
    And a hempen cord for my neck.

xxxix

Oh ! I would that I had never been born,
    To splendour and shame and sorrow,
For it's ill riding to grim Tiborne,
    Where I must ride to-morrow.

xl

I shall dress me all in silk and scarlet,
  And the hangman shall have my ring,
For though ,I be hanged like a low-born varlet
  They shall know I was once a king.

xli

And may I not fall faint or sick
  Till I reach at last to the goal,
And I pray that the rope may choke me quick
  And Christ receive my soul.

Hatch House, 1893.

A Song

Steal from the meadows, rob the tall green hills,
   Ravish my orchard's blossoms, let me bind
A crown of orchard flowers and daffodils,
   Because my love is fair and white and kind.

To-day the thrush has trilled her daintiest phrases,
   Flowers with their incense have made drunk the air,
God has bent down to gild the hearts of daisies,
   Because my love is kind and white and fair.

To-day the sun has kissed the rose-tree's daughter,
   And sad Narcissus, Spring's pale acolyte,
Hangs down his head and smiles into the water,
   Because my love is kind and fair and white.

Crabbet Park, 1894.

Plainte Eternelle

The sun sinks down, the tremulous daylight dies.
  (Down their long shafts the weary sunbeams glide.)
  The white-winged ships drift with the falling tide,
Come back, my love, with pity in your eyes !

The tall white ships drift with the falling tide.
  (Far, far away I hear the seamews' cries.)
  Come back, my love, with pity in your eyes !
There is no room now in my heart for pride.

Come back, come back ! with pity in your eyes.
  (The night is dark, the sea is fierce and wide.)
  There is no room now in my heart for pride,
Though I become the scorn of all the wise.

I have no place now in my heart for pride.
  (The moon and stars have fallen from the skies.)
  Though I become the scorn of all the wise,
Thrust, if you will, sharp arrows in my side.

Let me become the scorn of all the wise.
   (Out of the East I see the morning ride.)
   Thrust, if you will, sharp arrows in my side,
Play with my tears and feed upon my sighs.

Wound me with swords, put arrows in my side.
   (On the white sea the haze of noon-day lies.)
   Play with my tears and feed upon my sighs,
But come, my love, before my heart has died.

Drink my salt tears and feed upon my sighs.
   (Westward the evening goes with one red stride.)
   Come back, my love, before my heart has died,
Down sinks the sun, the tremulous daylight dies.

Come back ! my love, before my heart has died.
   (Out of the South I see the pale moon rise.)
   Down sinks the sun, the tremulous daylight dies,
The white-winged ships drift with the falling tide.

Jonquil and Fleur-de-lys

i

Jonquil was a shepherd lad,
    White he was as the curded cream,
Hair like the buttercups he had,
    And wet green eyes like a full chalk stream.

ii

His teeth were as white as the stones that lie
    Down in the depths of the sun-bright river,
And his lashes danced like a dragon-fly
    With drops on the gauzy wings that quiver.

iii

His lips were as red as round ripe cherries,
    And his delicate cheeks and his rose-pink neck
Were stained with the colour of dog-rose berries
    When they lie on the snow like a crimson fleck.

iv

His feet were all stained with the cowslips and grass
    To amber and verdigris,
And through his folds one day did pass
    The young prince Fleur-de-lys.

39

Fleur-de-lys was the son of the king.
 He was as white as an onyx stone,
His hair was curled like a daffodil ring,
 And his eyes were like gems in the queen's blue zone.

His teeth were as white as the white pearls set
 Round the thick white throat of the queen in the hall,
And his lashes were like the dark silk net
 That she binds her yellow hair withal.

His lips were as red as the red rubies
 The king's bright dagger-hilt that deck,
And pale rose-pink as the amethyst is
 Were his delicate cheeks and his rose-pink neck.

His feet were all shod in shoes of gold,
 And his coat was as gold as a blackbird's bill is,
With jewel on jewel manifold,
 And wrought with a pattern of golden lilies.

When Fleur-de-lys espied Jonquil
 He was as glad as a bird in May ;
He tripped right swiftly a-down the hill,
 And called to the shepherd boy to play.

This fell out ere the sheep-shearing,
  That these two lads did sport and toy,
Fleur-de-lys the son of the king,
  And sweet Jonquil the shepherd boy.

And after they had played awhile,
  Thereafter they to talking fell,
And full an hour they did beguile
  While each his state and lot did tell.

For Jonquil spake of the little sheep,
  And the tender ewes that know their names,
And he spake of his wattled hut for sleep,
  And the country sports and the shepherds' games.

And he plucked a reed from the edge that girds
  The river bank, and with his knife
Made a pipe, with a breath like the singing birds
  When they flute to their loves in a musical strife.

And he told of the night so long and still
  When he lay awake till he heard the feet
Of the goat-foot god coming over the hill,
  And the rustling sound as he passed through the wheat.

And Fleur-de-lys told of the king and the court,
　　And the stately dames and the slender pages,
Of his horse and his hawk and his mimic fort,
　　And the silent birds in their golden cages.

And the jewelled sword with the damask blade
　　That should be his in his fifteenth spring ;
And the silver sound that the gold horns made,
　　And the tourney lists and the tilting ring.

And after that they did devise
　　For mirth and sport, that each should wear
The other's clothes, and in this guise
　　Make play each other's parts to bear.

Whereon they stripped off all their clothes,
　　And when they stood up in the sun,
They were as like as one white rose
　　On one green stalk, to another one.

And when Jonquil as a prince was shown
　　And Fleur-de-lys as a shepherd lad,
Their mothers' selves would not have known
　　That each the other's habit had.

xx

And Jonquil walked like the son of a king
   With dainty steps and proud haut look ;
And Fleur-de-lys, that sweet youngling,
   Did push and paddle his feet in the brook.

xxi

And while they made play in this wise,
   Unto them all in haste did run,
Two lords of the court, with joyful cries,
   That long had sought the young king's son.

xxii

And to Jonquil they reverence made
   And said, " My lord, we are come from the king,
Who is sore vexed that thou hast strayed
   So far without a following."

xxiii

Then unto them said Fleur-de-lys
   " You do mistake, my lords, for know
That I am the son of the king, and this
   Is sweet Jonquil, my playfellow."

xxiv

Whereat one of these lords replied,
   " Thou lying knave, I'll make thee rue
Such saucy words." But Jonquil cried,
   " Nay, nay, my lord, 'tis even true."

43

Whereat these lords were sore distressed,
    And one made answer bending knee,
" My lord the prince is pleased to jest."
    But Jonquil answered, " Thou shalt see."

xxvi

Sure never yet so strange a thing
    As this before was seen,
That a shepherd was thought the son of a king,
    And a prince a shepherd boy to have been.

xxvii

" Now mark me well, my noble lord,
    A shepherd's feet go bare and cold,
Therefore they are all green from the sward,
    And the buttercup makes a stain of gold.

xxviii

" That I am Jonquil thus shalt thou know,
    And that this be very Fleur-de-lys
If his feet be like the driven snow,
    And mine like the amber and verdigris."

xxix

He lifted up the shepherd's frock
    That clothed the prince, and straight did show
That his naked feet all under his smock
    Were whiter than the driven snow.

XXX

He doffed the shoes and the clothes of silk
  That he had gotten from Fleur-de-lys,
And all the rest was as white as milk,
  But his feet were like amber and verdigris.

xxxi

With that they each took back his own,
  And when this second change was done,
As a shepherd boy was Jonquil shown
  And Fleur-de-lys the king's true son.

xxxii

By this the sun was low in the heaven,
  And Fleur-de-lys must ride away,
But ere he left, with kisses seven,
  He vowed to come another day.

Hatch House, 1894.

A Prayer

Often the western wind has sung to me,
There have been voices in the streams and meres,
And pitiful trees have told me, God, of Thee :
And I heard not. Oh ! open Thou mine ears.

The reeds have whispered low as I passed by,
" Be strong, O friend, be strong, put off vain fears,
Vex not thy soul with doubts, God cannot lie " :
And I heard not. Oh ! open Thou mine ears.

There have been many stars to guide my feet,
Often the delicate moon, hearing my sighs,
Has rent the clouds and shown a silver street ;
And I saw not. Oh ! open Thou mine eyes.

Angels have beckoned me unceasingly,
And walked with me ; and from the sombre skies
Dear Christ Himself has stretched out hands to me ;
And I saw not. Oh ! open Thou mine eyes.

Clouds, 1894.

46

In Memoriam

Francis Archibald Douglas

Viscount Drumlanrig

Killed by the Accidental Explosion of his gun,
October 18, 1894

Dear friend, dear brother, I have owed you this
Since many days, the tribute of a song.
Shall I cheat you who never did a wrong
To any man ? No, therefore though I miss
All art, all skill, in this short armistice
From my soul's war against the bitter throng
Of present woes, let these poor lines be strong
In love enough to bear a brother's kiss.

Dear saint, true knight, I cannot weep for you,
Nor if I could would I call back the breath
To your dear body ; God is very wise,
All that this year had in its womb He knew,
And, loving you, He sent His Son like Death,
To put His hand over your kind gray eyes.

1895.

The Image of Death

I carved an image coloured like the night,
Winged with huge wings, stern-browed and menacing,
With hair caught back, and diademed like a king.
The left hand held a sceptre, and the right
Grasped a sharp sword, the bitter marble lips
Were curled and proud ; the yellow topaz eyes
(Each eye a jewel) stared in fearful wise ;
The hard fierce limbs were bare, and from the hips
A scourge hung down.   And on the pedestal
I wrote these words, " O all things that have breath
This is the image of the great god Death,
Pour ye the wine and bind the coronal !
Pipe unto him with pipes and flute with flutes,
Woo him with flowers and spices odorous,
Let singing boys with lips mellifluous
Make madrigals and lull his ear with lutes.
Anon bring sighs and tears of harsh distress,
And weeping wounds ! so haply ye may move
A heart of stone, from breasts of hate suck love,
Or garner pity from the pitiless."

Vae Victis !

Here in this isle
The summer still lingers,
And Autumn's brown fingers
So busy the while
With the leaves in the north,
Are scarcely put forth
In this land where the sun still glows like an ember,
In mid-November.

In England it's cold,
And the yellow and red
Of October have fled ;
And the sun is wet gold
Like an emperor weeping,
When Death goes a-reaping
All through his empire, merciless comer,
The dead things of summer.

The sky has cried so
That the earth is all sodden,
With dead leaves in-trodden,
And the trees to and fro

Wave their arms in the air
In despair, in despair :
They are thinking of all the hot days that are over,
And the cows in the clover.

Here the roses are out,
And the sun at high noon
Makes the birds faint and swoon.
But the cricket's about
With his song, and the hum
Of the bees as they come
To feast at the honey-board laden and groaning,
Makes musical droning.

But vainly, alas !
Do I hide in the south,
Kiss close with my mouth
Red flowers, green grass,
For Autumn has found me
And thrown her arms round me.
She has breathed on my lips and I wander apart,
Dead leaves in my heart.
Capri, 1895.

The Garden of Death

There is an isle in an unfurrowed sea
That I wot of, whereon the whole year round
The apple-blossoms and the rosebuds be
In early blooming ; and a many sound
Of ten-stringed lute, and most mellifluous breath
Of silver flute, and mellow half-heard horn,
Making unmeasured music. Thither Death
Coming like Love, takes all things in the morn
Of tenderest life, and being a delicate god,
In his own garden takes each delicate thing
Unstained, unmellowed, immature, untrod,
Tremulous betwixt the summer and the spring :
The rosebud ere it come to be a rose,
The blossom ere it win to be a fruit,
The virginal snowdrop, and the dove that knows
Only one dove for lover ; all the loot
Of young soft things, and all the harvesting
Of unripe flowers. Never comes the moon
To matron fulness, here no child-bearing
Vexes desire, and the sun knows no noon.
But all the happy dwellers of that place
Are reckless children, gotten on Delight
By Beauty that is thrall to Death ; no grace,

No natural sweet they lack, a chrysolite
Of perfect beauty each. No wisdom comes
To mar their early folly, no false laws
Man-made for man, no mouthing prudence numbs
Their green unthought, or gives their licence pause ;
Young animals, young flowers, they live and grow,
And die before their sweet emblossomed breath
Has learnt to sigh save like a lover's. Oh !
How sweet is Youth, how delicate is Death !

To Sleep

Ah, Sleep, to me thou com'st not in the guise
Of one who brings good gifts to weary men,
Balm for bruised hearts and fancies alien
To unkind truth, and drying for sad eyes.
I dread the summons to that fierce assize
Of all my foes and woes, that waits me when
Thou makest my soul the unwilling denizen
Of thy dim troubled house where unrest lies.

My soul is sick with dreaming, let it rest.
False Sleep, thou hast conspired with Wakefulness,
I will not praise thee, I too long beguiled
With idle tales.   Where is thy soothing breast ?
Thy peace, thy poppies, thy forgetfulness ?
Where is thy lap for me so tired a child ?

Ode to My Soul

Rise up my soul !
Shake thyself from the dust.
Lift up thy head that wears an aureole,
Fulfil thy trust.
Out of the mire where they would trample thee
Make images of clay,
Whereon having breathed from thy divinity
Let them take mighty wings and soar away
    Right up to God.
Out of thy broken past
Where impious feet have trod,
Build thee a golden house august and vast,
Whereto these worms of earth may some day crawl.
Let there be nothing small
Henceforth with thee ;
Take thou unbounded scorn of all their scorn,
    Eternity
Of high contempt : be thou no more forlorn
But proud in thy immortal loneliness,
And infinite distress :
And, being 'mid mortal things divinely born,
Rise up my soul !

Paris, 1896.

Rejected

Alas ! I have lost my God,
  My beautiful God Apollo.
Wherever his footsteps trod
  My feet were wont to follow.

But Oh ! it fell out one day
  My soul was so heavy with weeping,
That I laid me down by the way ;
  And he left me while I was sleeping.

And my soul awoke in the night,
  And I bowed my ear for his fluting,
And I heard but the breath of the flight
  Of wings and the night-birds hooting.

And night drank all her cup,
  And I went to the shrine in the hollow,
And the voice of my cry went up :
  " Apollo ! Apollo ! Apollo ! "

But he never came to the gate,
  And the sun was hid in a mist,
And there came one walking late,
  And I knew it was Christ.

He took my soul and bound it
　　With cords of iron wire,
Seven times round He wound it
　　With the cords of my desire.

The cords of my desire,
　　While my desire slept,
Were seven bands of wire
　　To bind my soul that wept.

And He hid my soul at last
　　In a place of stones and fears,
Where the hours like days went past
　　And the days went by like years.

And after many days
　　That which had slept awoke,
And desire burnt in a blaze,
　　And my soul went up in the smoke.

And we crept away from the place
　　And would not look behind,
And the angel that hides his face
　　Was crouched on the neck of the wind.

And I went to the shrine in the hollow
　　Where the lutes and the flutes were playing,
And cried : " I am come, Apollo,
　　Back to thy shrine, from my straying."

But he would have none of my soul
 That was stained with blood and with tears,
That had lain in the earth like a mole,
 In the place of great stones and fears.

And now I am lost in the mist
 Of the things that can never be,
For I will have none of Christ
 And Apollo will none of me.

Paris, 1896.

The Travelling Companion

Into the silence of the empty night
I went, and took my scornèd heart with me,
And all the thousand eyes of heaven were bright ;
But Sorrow came and led me back to thee.

I turned my weary eyes towards the sun,
Out of the leaden East like smoke came he.
I laughed and said, " The night is past and done " ;
But Sorrow came and led me back to thee.

I turned my face towards the rising moon,
Out of the south she came most sweet to see,
She smiled upon my eyes that loathed the noon ;
But Sorrow came and led me back to thee.

I bent my eyes upon the summer land,
And all the painted fields were ripe for me,
And every flower nodded to my hand ;
But Sorrow came and led me back to thee.

O Love ! O Sorrow ! O desired Despair !
I turned my feet towards the boundless sea,
Into the dark I go and heed not where,
So that I come again at last to thee.

The Legend of Spinello of Arezzo

Spinello of Arezzo long ago,
A cunning painter, made a large design
To grace the choir of St. Angelo.
Therein he pictured the exploits divine
Of the Archangel Michael, beautiful
Exceedingly, in wrath most terrible,
Until at last that holy place was full
Of warring angels ; and that one who fell
From the high places of the highest Heaven
Into the deep abyss of lowest Hell,
He pictured too, in mad disaster driven
Before the conquering hosts of Paradise.
And him the painter drew in uncouth shape,
A foul misshapen monster with fierce eyes,
Of hideous form, half demon and half ape.

And lo ! it fell out as he slept one night,
His soul, in the sad neutral land of dreams
That lies between the darkness and the light,
Was 'ware of one whose eyes were soft as beams
Of summer moonlight, and withal as sad.
Dark was his colour, and as black his hair
As hyacinths by night, his sweet lips had

A curve as piteous as sweet lovers wear
When they have lost their loves ; so fair was he,
So melancholy, yet withal so proud,
He seemed a prince whose woes might move a tree
To find a fearful voice and weep aloud.
He spoke, his voice was tunable and mellow,
But soft as are the western winds that stir
The summer leaves, and thus he said, " Spinello,
Why dost thou wrong me ? I am Lucifer."

Spring

Wake up again, sad heart, wake up again !
(I heard the birds this morning singing sweet.)
Wake up again ! The sky was crystal clear,
     And washed quite clean with rain ;
And far below my heart stirred with the year,
Stirred with the year and sighed. O pallid feet
Move now at last, O heart that sleeps with pain
     Rise up and hear
The voices in the valleys, run to meet
The songs and shadows. O wake up again !

Put out green leaves, dead tree, put out green
    leaves !
(Last night the moon was soft and kissed the air.)
Put out green leaves ! The moon was in the skies,
     All night she wakes and weaves.
The dew was on the grass like fairies' eyes,
Like fairies' eyes. O tree so black and bare,
Remember all the fruits, the full gold sheaves ;
     For nothing dies,
The songs that are, are silences that were,
Summer was Winter. O put out green leaves !

Break through the earth, pale flower, break through the
    earth !
(All day the lark has sung a madrigal.)
Break through the earth that lies not lightly yet
    And waits thy patient birth,
Waits for the jonquil and the violet,
The violet. Full soon the heavy pall
Will be a bed, and in the noon of mirth
    Some rivulet
Will bubble in my wilderness, some call
Will touch my silence. O break through the earth.

Ennui

Alas ! and oh that Spring should come again
Upon the soft wings of desired days,
And bring with her no anodyne to pain,
And no discernment of untroubled ways.
There was a time when her yet distant feet,
Guessed by some prescience more than half divine,
Gave to my listening ear such happy warning,
    That fresh, serene, and sweet,
My thoughts soared up like larks into the morning,
From the dew-sprinkled meadows crystalline.

Soared up into the heights celestial,
And saw the whole world like a ball of fire,
Fashioned to be a monster playing ball
For the enchantment of my young desire.
And yesterday they flew to this black cloud,
(Missing the way to those ethereal spheres.)
And saw the earth a vision of affright,
    And men a sordid crowd,
And felt the fears and drank the bitter tears,
And saw the empty houses of Delight.

The sun has sunk into a moonless sea,
And every road leads down from Heaven to Hell,
The pearls are numbered on youth's rosary,
I have outlived the days desirable.
What is there left ?   And how shall dead men sing
Unto the loosened strings of Love and Hate,
Or take strong hands to Beauty's ravishment ?
        Who shall devise this thing,
To give high utterance to Miscontent,
Or make Indifference articulate ?

Wine of Summer

The sun holds all the earth and all the sky
From the gold throne of this midsummer day.
In the soft air the shadow of a sigh
Breathes on the leaves and scarcely makes them sway.
The wood lies silent in the shimmering heat,
Save where the insects make a lazy drone,
And ever and anon from some tree near,
     A dove's enamoured moan,
Or distant rook's faint cawing harsh and sweet,
Comes dimly floating to my listening ear.

Right in the wood's deep heart I lay me down,
And look up at the sky between the leaves,
Through delicate lace I see her deep blue gown.
Across a fern a scarlet spider weaves
From branch to branch a slender silver thread,
And hangs there shining in the white sunbeams,
A ruby tremulous on a streak of light.
     And high above my head
One spray of honeysuckle sways and dreams,
With one wild honey-bee for acolyte.

My nest is all untrod and virginal,
And virginal the path that led me here,
For all along the grass grew straight and tall,
And live things rustled in the thicket near :
And briar rose stretched out to sweet briar rose
Wild slender arms, and barred the way to me
With many a flowering arch, rose-pink or white,
      As bending carefully,
Leaving unbroken all their blossoming bows,
I passed along, a reverent neophyte.

The air is full of soft imaginings,
They float unseen beneath the hot sunbeams,
Like tired moths on heavy velvet wings.
They droop above my drowsy head like dreams.
The hum of bees, the murmuring of doves,
The soft faint whispering of unnumbered trees,
Mingle with unreal things, and low and deep
      From visionary groves,
Imagined lutes make voiceless harmonies,
And false flutes sigh before the gates of sleep.

O rare sweet hour ! O cup of golden wine !
The night of these my days is dull and dense,
And stars are few, be this the anodyne !
Of many woes the perfect recompense.
I thought that I had lost for evermore

The sense of this ethereal drunkenness,
This fierce desire to live, to breathe, to be ;
        But even now, no less
Than in the merry noon that danced before
My tedious night, I taste its ecstasy.

Taste, and remember all the summer days
That lie, like golden reflections in the lake
Of vanished years, unreal but sweet always ;
Soft luminous shadows that I may not take
Into my hands again, but still discern
Drifting like gilded ghosts before my eyes,
Beneath the waters of forgotten things,
        Sweet with faint memories,
And mellow with old loves that used to burn
Dead summer days ago, like fierce red kings.

And this hour too must die, even now the sun
Droops to the sea, and with untroubled feet
The quiet evening comes : the day is done.
The air that throbbed beneath the passionate heat
Grows calm and cool and virginal again.
The colour fades and sinks to sombre tones,
As when in youthful cheeks a blush grows dim.
        Hushed are the monotones
Of doves and bees, and the long flowery lane
Rustles beneath the wind in playful whim.

Gone are the passion and the pulse that beat
With fevered strokes, and gone the unseen things
That clothed the hour with shining raiment meet
To deck enchantments and imaginings.
No joy is here but only neutral peace
And loveless languor and indifference,
And faint remembrance of lost ecstasy.
    The darkening shades increase,
My dreams go out like tapers—I must hence.
Far off I hear Night calling to the sea.

Ode to Autumn

Thou sombre lady of down-bended head,
And weary lashes drooping to the cheek,
With sweet sad fold of lips uncomforted,
And listless hands more tired with strife than meek;
Turn here thy soft brown feet, and to my heart,
Unmatched to Summer's golden minstrelsy,
Or Spring's shrill pipe of joy, sing once again
      Sad songs, and I to thee
Well tuned, will answer that according part
That jarred with those young seasons' gladder strain.

Give me thy empty branches for the biers
Of perished joys, thy winds to sigh my sighs,
Thy falling leaves to count my falling tears,
And all thy mists to dim my aching eyes.
There is no comfort in thy lips, and none
In thy cold arms, nor pity in thy breast,
But better 'tis in gray hours to have grief,
      Than to affront the sun
With sunless woe, when every flower and leaf
Conspires to make the season merriest.

The drip of rain-drops on the sodden earth,
The trampled mud-stained grass, the shifting leaves,
The silent hurrying birds, the sickly birth
Of the red sun in misty skies, the sheaves
Of rotting ruined corn, the sudden gusts
Of angry winds, the clouds that fly all night
Before the stormy moon, thy desolate moans,
  All thy decays and rusts,
Thy deaths and dirges, these are tuned aright
To my unquiet soul that sorrow owns.

But ah ! thy gentler mood, the honeyed kiss
Of thy faint watery sunshine, thy pale gold,
Thy dark red berries, and the ambergris
That paints the lingering leaves, while on the mould,
Their dead make bronze and sepia carpetings
That lightly rustle in thy quiet breath.
These are the shadows of departed smiles,
  The ghosts of happy things ;
These break again the broken heart, the whiles
Thou goest on to winter, I to Death.

Harmonie du Soir

(From the French of Baudelaire)

Voici venir le temps.

Now is the hour when, swinging in the breeze,
Each flower, like a censer, sheds its sweet.
The air is full of scents and melodies,
O languorous waltz ! O swoon of dancing feet !

Each flower, like a censer, sheds its sweet,
The violins are like sad souls that cry,
O languorous waltz ! O swoon of dancing feet !
A shrine of Death and Beauty is the sky.

The violins are like sad souls that cry,
Poor souls that hate the vast black night of Death ;
A shrine of Death and Beauty is the sky.
Drowned in red blood, the Sun gives up his breath.

This soul that hates the vast black night of Death
Takes all the luminous past back tenderly,
Drowned in red blood, the Sun gives up his breath.
Thine image like a monstrance shines in me.

71

Le Balcon

(From the French of Baudelaire)

Mère des souvenirs, maîtresses des maîtresses.

Mother of Memories ! O mistress-queen !
Oh ! all my joy and all my duty thou !
The beauty of caresses that have been,
The evenings and the hearth remember now,
Mother of Memories ! O mistress-queen !

The evenings burning with the glowing fire,
And on the balcony, the rose-stained nights !
How sweet, how kind you were, my soul's desire.
We said things wonderful as chrysolites,
When evening burned beside the glowing fire.

How fair the Sun is in the evening !
How strong the soul, how high the heaven's high tower !
O first and last of every worshipped thing,
Your odorous heart's-blood filled me like a flower.
How fair the sun is in the evening !

The night grew deep between us like a pall,
And in the dark I guessed your shining eyes,

72

And drank your breath, O sweet, O honey-gall!
Your little feet slept on me sister-wise.
The night grew deep between us like a pall.

I can call back the days desirable,
And live all bliss again between your knees,
For where else can I find that magic spell
Save in your heart and in your Mysteries?
I can call back the days desirable.

These vows, these scents, these kisses infinite,
Will they like young suns climbing up the skies
Rise up from some unfathomable pit,
Washed in the sea from all impurities?
O vows, O scents, O kisses infinite!

The Ballad of Saint Vitus

Vitus came tripping over the grass
When all the leaves in the trees were green,
Through the green meadows he did pass
On the day he was full seventeen.

The lark was singing up over his head,
As he went by so lithe and fleet,
And the flowers danced in white and red
At the treading of his nimble feet.

His neck was as brown as the brown earth is
When first the young brown plough-boys delve it,
And his lips were as red as mulberries
And his eyes were like the soft black velvet.

His silk brown hair was touched with bronze,
And his brown cheeks had the tender hue
That like a dress the brown earth dons
When the pink carnations bloom anew.

He was slim as the reeds that sway all along
The banks of the lake, and as straight as a rush,
And as he passed he sang a song,
And his voice was as sweet as the voice of a thrush.

He sang of the Gardens of Paradise,
And the light of God that never grows dim,
And the Cherubim with their radiant eyes,
And the rainbow wings of the Seraphim.

And the host as countless as all days,
That worships there, and ceases not,
Singing and praising God always,
With lute and flute and angelot.

And the blessèd light of Mary's face
As she sits among these pleasant sounds,
And Christ that is the Prince of Grace,
And the five red flowers that be His wounds.

And so he went till he came to the doors
Of the ivory house of his father the King,
And all through the golden corridors,
As he passed along, he ceased to sing.

But a pagan priest had seen him pass,
And heard his voice as he went along
Through the fields of the bending grass,
And he heard the words of the holy song.

And he sought the King where he sat on his throne,
And the tears of wrath were in his eyes,
And he said, " O Sire, be it known
That thy son singeth in this wise :

" Of the blessèd light of Mary's face
As she sits amidst sweet pleasant sounds,
And how that Christ is the Prince of Grace,
And hath five flowers that be His wounds."

And when the King had heard this thing,
His brow grew black as a winter night,
And he bade the pages seek and bring
Straightway the prince before his sight.

And Vitus came before the King,
And the King cried out, " I pray thee, son,
Sing now the song that thou didst sing
When thou cam'st through the fields anon."

And the face of the prince grew white as milk,
And he answered nought, but under the band
That held his doublet of purple silk
Round his slight waist, he thrust his hand.

And the King picked up a spear, and cried,
" What hast thou there ? by the waters of Styx,
Speak or I strike," and the boy replied,
" Sweet Sire, it is a crucifix."

And the King grew black with rage and grief,
And for a full moment he spake no word.
And the spear in his right hand shook like a leaf,
And the vein on his brow was a tight blue cord.

Then he laughed and said, in bitter scorn,
" Take me this Christian fool from my sight,
Lock him in the turret till the morn,
And let him dance alone to-night.

" He shall sit in the dark while the courtly ball
All the gay night sweeps up and down
On the polished floor of the golden hall,
And thus shall he win his martyr's crown."

Thus spake the King, and the courtiers smiled,
And Vitus hung his head for shame ;
And he thought, " I am punished like a child,
That would have died for Christ's dear Name."

And so 'twas done, and on that night,
While silk and sword, with fan and flower,
Danced in the hall in the golden light,
Prince Vitus sat in the lone dark tower.

But the King bethought him, and was moved,
Ere the short summer night was done,
And his heart's blood yearned for the son he loved,
His dainty prince, his only son.

And all alone he climbed the stair,
With the tired feet of a sceptred King,
And came to the door, and lo ! he was 'ware
Of the sound of flute and lute-playing.

And as the King stood there amazed,
The iron door flew open wide,
And the King fell down on his knees as he gazed
At the wondrous thing he saw inside.

For the room was filled with a soft sweet light
Of ambergris and apricot,
And round the walls were angels bright,
With lute and flute and angelot.

On lute and angelot they played,
With their gold heads bowed upon the strings,
And the soft wind that the slim flutes made,
Stirred in the feathers of their wings.

And in the midst serene and sweet
With God's light on his countenance
Was Vitus, with his gold shod feet,
Dancing in a courtly dance.

And round him were archangels four,
Michael, who guards God's citadel,
Raphael, whom children still implore,
And Gabriel and Uriel.

Thus long ago was Christ's behest,
And the saving grace that His red wounds be,
Unto this king made manifest,
And all his land of Sicily.

God sits within the highest Heaven,
His mercy neither tires nor faints,
All good gifts that may be given,
He gives unto His holy Saints.

This was the joy that Vitus gat ;
To dance with Angels knee by knee,
Before he came to man's estate :
God send us all such Company.

                              Amen.

                    Aix-Les-Bains, 1897.

The City of the Soul

i

In the salt terror of a stormy sea
There are high altitudes the mind forgets ;
And undesired days are hunting nets
To snare the souls that fly Eternity.
But we being gods will never bend the knee,
Though sad moons shadow every sun that sets,
And tears of sorrow be like rivulets
To feed the shallows of Humility.

Within my soul are some mean gardens found
Where drooped flowers are, and unsung melodies,
And all companioning of piteous things.
But in the midst is one high terraced ground,
Where level lawns sweep through the stately trees
And the great peacocks walk like painted kings.

ii

What shall we do, my soul, to please the King ?
Seeing he hath no pleasure in the dance,
And hath condemned the honeyed utterance
Of silver flutes and mouths made round to sing.

Along the wall red roses climb and cling,
And oh ! my prince, lift up thy countenance,
For there be thoughts like roses that entrance
More than the languors of soft lute-playing.

Think how the hidden things that poets see
In amber eves or mornings crystalline,
Hide in the soul their constant quenchless light,
Till, called by some celestial alchemy,
Out of forgotten depths, they rise and shine
Like buried treasure on Midsummer night.

iii

The fields of Phantasy are all too wide,
My soul runs through them like an untamed thing.
It leaps the brooks like threads, and skirts the ring
Where fairies danced, and tenderer flowers hide.
The voice of music has become the bride
Of an imprisoned bird with broken wing.
What shall we do, my soul, to please the King,
We that are free, with ample wings untied ?

We cannot wander through the empty fields
Till beauty like a hunter hurl the lance.
There are no silver snares and springes set,
Nor any meadow where the plain ground yields.
O let us then with ordered utterance,
Forge the gold chain and twine the silken net.

iv

Each new hour's passage is the acolyte
Of inarticulate song and syllable,
And every passing moment is a bell,
To mourn the death of undiscerned delight.
Where is the sun that made the noon-day bright,
And where the midnight moon ? O let us tell,
In long carved line and painted parable,
How the white road curves down into the night.

Only to build one crystal barrier
Against this sea which beats upon our days ;
To ransom one lost moment with a rhyme
Or if fate cries and grudging gods demur,
To clutch Life's hair, and thrust one naked phrase
Like a lean knife between the ribs of Time.

Naples, 1897.

Sonnet on the Sonnet

To see the moment holds a madrigal,
To find some cloistered place, some hermitage
For free devices, some deliberate cage
Wherein to keep wild thoughts like birds in thrall ;
To eat sweet honey and to taste black gall,
To fight with form, to wrestle and to rage,
Till at the last upon the conquered page
The shadows of created Beauty fall.

This is the sonnet, this is all delight
Of every flower that blows in every Spring,
And all desire of every desert place ;
This is the joy that fills a cloudy night
When, bursting from her misty following,
A perfect moon wins to an empty space.

A Triad of the Moon

i

Last night my window played with one moonbeam,
And I lay watching till sleep came, and stole
Over my eyelids, and she brought a shoal
Of hurrying thoughts that were her troubled team,
And in the weary ending of a dream
I found this word upon a candid scroll :
" The nightingale is like a poet's soul,
She finds fierce pain in miseries that seem."

Ah me, methought, that she should so devise !
To seek for pain and sing such doleful bars,
That the wood aches and simple flowers cry,
And sea-green tears drench mortal lovers' eyes,
She that is made the lure of those young stars
That hang like golden spiders in the sky.

ii

That she should so devise, to find such lore
Of sighful song and piteous psalmody,
While Joy runs on through summer greenery,
And all Delight is like an open door.

84

Must then her liquid notes for evermore
Repeat the colour of sad things, and be
Distilled like cassia drops of agony,
From the slow anguish of a heart's bruised core ?

Nay, she weeps not because she knows sad songs,
But sings because she weeps ; for wilful food
Of her sad singing, she will still decoy
The sweetness that to happy things belongs.
All night with artful woe she holds the wood.
And all the summer day with natural joy.

iii

My soul is like a silent nightingale
Devising sorrow in a summer night.
Closed eyes in blazing noon put out the light,
And Hell lies in the thickness of a veil.
In every voiceless moment sleeps a wail,
And all the lonely darknesses are bright,
And every dawning of the day is white
With shapes of sorrow fugitive and frail.

My soul is like a flower whose honey-bees
Are pains that sting and suck the sweets untold,
My soul is like an instrument of strings ;
I must stretch these to capture harmonies,
And to find songs like buried dust of gold,
Delve with the nightingale for sorrowful things.

Proem

How have we fared my soul across the days,
Through what green valleys, confident and fleet,
Along what paths of flint with how tired feet ?
Anon we knew the terror that dismays
At noonday ; and when night made dark the ways
We bought delight and found remembrance sweet.
Though in our ears we heard the wide wings beat
Ever we kept dumb mouths to prayer and praise.

Yet never lost or spurned or cast aside,
And never sundered from the love of God,
Through how-so wayward intricate deceits,
Lured by what shining toys, our charmed feet trod,
On the swift winds we saw bright angels ride,
And strayed into the moon-made silver streets.

1910.

86

Dedication to "Sonnets" (1909)

What shall I say, what word, what cry recall,
What god invoke, what star, what amulet,
To make a sonnet pay a hopeless debt,
Or bind a winged heart with a madrigal?
Weak words are vainer than no words at all,
The barrier of flesh divides us yet;
Your spirit, like a bird caught in a net,
Beats ever an impenetrable wall.

This is my book, and there as in a glass,
Darkly beheld, the shadow of my mind
Wavers and flickers like a flame of fire.
So through your eyes, it may be, it will pass,
And I shall hold my wild shy bird confined
In the gold cage of shadowless desire.

The Dead Poet

I dreamed of him last night, I saw his face
All radiant and unshadowed of distress,
And as of old, in music measureless,
I heard his golden voice and marked him trace
Under the common thing the hidden grace,
And conjure wonder out of emptiness,
Till mean things put on beauty like a dress
And all the world was an enchanted place.

And then methought outside a fast locked gate
I mourned the loss of unrecorded words,
Forgotten tales and mysteries half said,
Wonders that might have been articulate,
And voiceless thoughts like murdered singing birds.
And so I woke and knew that he was dead.

Paris, 1901.

Dies Amara Valde

Ah me, ah me, the day when I am dead,
And all of me that was immaculate
Given to darkness, lies in shame or state,
Surely my soul shall come to that last bed
And weep for all the whiteness that was red,
Standing beside the ravished ivory gate
When the pale dwelling-place is desolate
And all the golden rooms untenanted.

For in the smoke of that last holocaust,
When to the regions of unsounded air
That which is deathless still aspires and tends,
Whither my helpless soul shall we be tossed?
To what disaster of malign Despair,
Or terror of unfathomable ends?

1902.

To a Silent Poet

Where are the eagle-wings that lifted thee
Above the ken of mortal hopes and fears,
And was it thou who in serener years
Framed magic words with such sweet symmetry?
Didst thou compel the sun, the stars, the sea,
Harness the golden horses of the spheres,
And make the winds of God thy charioteers
Along the roads of Immortality?

Art thou dead then?   Nay, leave the folded scroll,
Let us keep quiet lips and patient hands,
Not as sheer children use, who would unclose
The petals of young flowers, but paying toll
At that high gate where Time grave gardener, stands
Waiting the ripe fulfilment of the rose.

The Traitor

Cast out my soul the broken covenant,
Forget the pitiable masquerade,
And that ignoble part ignobly played.
Let us take shame that such a mummer's rant
Of noble things, could pierce the adamant
Of Pride wherewith we ever were arrayed,
And being with a kiss once more betrayed,
Let not our tears honour that sycophant.

Let him, on graves of buried loyalty,
Rise as he may to his desired goal ;
Ay and God speed him here, I grudge him not.
And when all men shall sing his praise to me
I'll not gainsay.   But I shall know his soul
Lies in the bosom of Iscariot.

Beauty and the Hunter

Where lurks the shining quarry, swift and shy,
Immune, elusive, unsubstantial ?
In what dim forests of the soul, where call
No birds, and no beasts creep ? (the hunter's cry
Wounds the deep darkness, and the low winds sigh
Through avenues of trees whose faint leaves fall
Down to the velvet ground, and like a pall
The violet shadows cover all the sky).

With what gold nets, what silver-pointed spears
May we surprise her, what slim flutes inspire
With breath of what serene enchanted air ?—
Wash we our star-ward gazing eyes with tears,
Till on their pools (drawn by our white desire)
She bend and look, and leave her image there.

Rewards

From the beginning, when was aught but stones
For English Prophets ?   Starved not Chatterton ?
Was Keats bay-crowned, was Shelley smiled upon ?
Marlowe died timely. Well for him, his groans
On stake or rack else had out-moaned the moans
Of his own Edward ; and that light that shone,
That voice, that trumpet, that white-throated swan,
When found he praise, save for " his honoured bones " ?

Honour enough for bones ! but for live flesh
Cold-eyed mistrust, and ever watchful fear,
Mingled with homage given grudgingly
From cautious mouths. And all the while a mesh
To snare the singing-bird, to trap the deer,
And bind the feet of Immortality.

The Academy Office, 1908.

Silence

This is a deep hell, to be expressionless,
To leave emotion inarticulate,
To guess some form of Love or Joy or Hate
Shadowed in an imperial loveliness
Behind the hurrying thoughts that crowd and press,
To track, to follow, to lie down, to wait,
And at the last before some fearful gate
To stand eluded and companionless.

Oh, if proud summer's high magnificence
And all the garnered honey of sweet days,
And sweets of sweeter nights, cannot prevail
Against this spell of tongue-tied impotence,
How shall we sing my soul when skies are pale,
And winter suns shed melancholy rays?

The Green River

I know a green grass path that leaves the field,
And like a running river, winds along
Into a leafy wood where is no throng
Of birds at noon-day, and no soft throats yield
Their music to the moon. The place is sealed,
An unclaimed sovereignty of voiceless song,
And all the unravished silences belong
To some sweet singer lost or unrevealed.

So is my soul become a silent place.
Oh may I wake from this uneasy night
To find a voice of music manifold.
Let it be shape of sorrow with wan face,
Or Love that swoons on sleep, or else delight
That is as wide-eyed as a marigold.

La Beauté

(*From the French of Baudelaire*)

Fair am I, mortals, as a stone-carved dream,
And all men wound themselves against my breast,
The poet's last desire, the loveliest.
Voiceless, eternal as the world I seem.
In the blue air, strange sphinx, I brood supreme
With heart of snow whiter than swan's white crest,
No movement mars the plastic line—I rest
With lips untaught to laugh or eyes to stream.

Singers who see, in trancèd interludes,
My splendour set with all superb design,
Consume their days, in toilful ecstasy.
To these revealed, the starry amplitudes
Of my great eyes which make all things divine
Are crystal mirrors of eternity.

Sois Sage O Ma Douleur

(From the French of Baudelaire)

Peace, be at peace, O thou my heaviness,
Thou calledst for the evening, lo ! 'tis here,
The City wears a sombre atmosphere
That brings repose to some, to some distress.
Now while the heedless throng make haste to press
Where pleasure drives them, ruthless charioteer,
To pluck the fruits of sick remorse and fear,
Come thou with me, and leave their fretfulness.

See how they hang from heaven's high balconies,
The old lost years in worn clothes garmented,
And see Regret with faintly smiling mouth ;
And while the dying sun sinks in the skies,
Hear how, far off, Night walks with velvet tread,
And her long robe trails all about the south.

To Olive

When in dim dreams I trace the tangled maze
Of the old years that held and fashioned me,
And to the sad assize of Memory
From the wan roads and misty time-trod ways,
The timid ghosts of dead forgotten days
Gather to hold their piteous colloquy,
Chiefly my soul bemoans the lack of thee
And those lost seasons empty of thy praise.

Yet surely thou wast there when life was sweet,
(We walked knee-deep in flowers) and thou wast there,
When in dismay and sorrow and unrest,
With weak bruised hands and wounded bleeding feet,
I fought with beasts and wrestled with despair
And slept (how else?) upon thine unseen breast.

I have been profligate of happiness
And reckless of the world's hostility,
The blessèd part has not been given to me
Gladly to suffer fools, I do confess

I have enticed and merited distress,
By this, that I have never bowed the knee
Before the shrine of wise Hypocrisy,
Nor worn self-righteous anger like a dress.

Yet write you this, sweet one, when I am dead :
" Love like a lamp swayed over all his days
And all his life was like a lamp-lit chamber,
Where is no nook, no chink unvisited
By the soft affluence of golden rays,
And all the room is bathed in liquid amber."

iii

Long, long ago you lived in Italy,
You were a little princess in a state
Where all things sweet and strange did congregate,
And in your eyes was hope or memory
Or wistful prophecy of things to be ;
You gave a child's blank " no " to proffered fate,
Then became grave, and died immaculate,
Leaving torn hearts and broken minstrelsy.

But Love that weaves the years on Time's slow loom
Found you again, reborn, fashioned and grown
To your old likeness in these harsher lands ;
And when life's day was shadowed in deep gloom
You found me wandering, heart-sick and alone,
And ran to me and gave me both your hands.

My thoughts like bees explore all sweetest things
To fill for you the honeycomb of praise,
Linger in roses and white jasmine sprays,
And marigolds that stand in yellow rings.
In the blue air they moan on muted strings,
And the blue sky of my soul's summer days
Shines with your light, and through pale violet ways,
Birds bear your name in beatings of their wings.

I see you all bedecked in bows of rain,
New showers of rain against new-risen suns,
New tears against new light of shining joy.
My youth, equipped to go, turns back again,
Throws down its heavy pack of years and runs
Back to the golden house a golden boy.

v

When we were Pleasure's minions, you and I,
When we mocked grief and held disaster cheap,
And shepherded all joys like willing sheep
That love their shepherd ; when a passing sigh
Was all the cloud that flecked our April sky,
I floated on an unimagined deep,
I loved you as a tired child loves sleep,
I lived and laughed and loved, and knew not why.

Now I have known the uttermost rose of love ;
The years are very long, but love is longer ;
I love you so, I have no time to hate
Even those wolves without. The great winds move
All their dark batteries to our fragile gate :
The world is very strong, but love is stronger.

vi

When I am dead you shall not doubt or fear,
Or wander nightly in the halls of gloom.
The moon will shine into my empty room,
And in the narrow garden flowers will peer,
While you look through your window. Scarce a tear
Will drench your child's blue eyes, while on my tomb,
Where the red roses wake and break and bloom,
The stars gaze down eternal and austere.

And I, in the dark ante-room of Death,
Will wait for you with ever-outstretched hands
And ears strained for your little timid feet ;
And in the listening darkness, when your breath
Pants in distress, my arms will be like bands
And all my weakness like your winding-sheet.

1907.

Forgetfulness

Alas ! that Time should war against Distress,
And numb the sweet ache of remembered loss,
And give for sorrow's gold the indifferent dross
Of calm regret or stark forgetfulness.
I should have worn eternal mourning dress
And nailed my soul to some perennial cross,
And made my thoughts like restless waves that toss
On the wild sea's intemperate wilderness.

But lo ! came Life, and with its painted toys
Lured me to play again like any child.
O pardon me this weak inconstancy.
May my soul die if in all present joys,
Lapped in forgetfulness or sense-beguiled
Yea, in my mirth, if I prefer not thee.

Premonition

If Love reveal himself, to haggard eyes,
Compact of lust and curiosity,
And turn a pallid face away from thee
To seek elsewhere a harlot's paradise ;
If Faith be perjured and if Truth be lies,
And thy great oak of life a rotten tree,
Where shall we hide, my soul, how shall we flee
The eternal fire, the worm that never dies ?

O born to be rejected and denied,
Scorn of the years and sport of all the days,
Must the gray future still repeat the past ?
O thrice betrayed and seven times crucified,
Is there no issue from unhappy ways,
No peace, no hope, no loving arms at last ?

La Brague, 1903.

The Witch

You cannot build again what you have broken,
You cannot bind the words your lips have spoken.

You broke the golden bowl and shattered it,
You put away Remembrance in a pit.

You sprinkled earth, you wove a spell and sang,
And on its grave certain red lilies sprang.

You watered them with a betrayed man's tears,
And found them fair. God sent you sighs and fears.

You bent them to your lust and made them be
Food for your Hell-imagined ecstasy.

You took Remorse and strangled it by night,
And sank it in a well. You bound Delight

And brought it home : the cord that held it fast
Was the forgetfulness of kindness past.

You took the price of him you had betrayed
And bought you toys and decked yourself and played

Like any child : you were all soft and sweet ;
Your lovers watched your little dancing feet

With glowing eyes, too lover-blind to see
In your white hands clasped close the Judas fee.

You took the price and you have held it still ;
And now, far off, you see Heaven on a hill,

And dream of peace and gates of pearl unlocked—
Poor fool ! be not deceived, God is not mocked.

1915.

Behold, Your House is Left Unto You Desolate

Alas, for Love and Truth and Faith, stone dead,
Borne down by Hate to death unnatural,
Stifled and poisoned ! From the empty hall
To the dismantled chamber where the bed
Once held its breathing warmth, the soundless tread
Of sad ghosts goes by night. Timid and small
One creeps and glides ; I saw her shadow fall
Behind me on the floor uncarpeted.

Poor wistful semblance of too weak remorse
Why have we met in your forsaken room,
Where the pale moon looks in on emptiness
And holds a lamp to ruin ? Fragile force
You come too late, my cold heart is a tomb
Where love lies strangled in his wedding dress.

26 Church Row, 1913.

The End of Illusion

" And for thou wast a spirit too delicate
  To act her earthy and abhorred commands,
  Refusing her grand hests, she did confine thee
  Into a cloven pine ; within which rift
  Imprisoned, thou didst painfully remain
  A dozen years." *

The Tempest, Act I, Sc. 2.

How wretchedly have I with trancèd eyes
(Chained galley-slaves of Hell-born sorcery)
Gazed on this world as through a shallow sea
Or glass of coloured jewels. Who is wise
That looks to find on earth a paradise ?
Or how shall the flame-cinctured spirit go free
That's harnessed to a fleshly sovereignty,
Or gold-wired in a cage of woman's lies ?

You were all Juliet and Rosalind
And Imogen to me. You snared my soul
And would have moulded it like pliant wax
Into the image of your lust, your mind
Is like Hell's furnace full of burning coal.
I know you now, Circe and Sycorax.

Hesdigneul, 1914.

* 1902–1914.

Canker Blooms

" But for their virtue only is their show,
They live unwooed and unrespected fade."
SHAKESPEARE, *Sonnet* 54.

Alas that evil things should find this gift,
To be so housed and so caparisoned,
So lapped in silk and so pavilioned
In such sweet tents, that we who darkly lift
Our still illusioned eyes know not to sift
The soaring noble from the falsely fond.
While Virtue like a needy vagabond
With unadmired demeanour makes rude shift.

You were all fair without, not so within.
I looked at you and loved you. Your bright shell
Was opal-hued but not inhabited
By honourable jewels. Like a sin
You charmed my soul, but ere we came to Hell
Love died.—Let now the dead entomb their dead.

1916.

The Unspeakable Englishman

You were a brute and more than half a knave,
Your mind was seamed with labyrinthine tracks
Wherein walked crazy moods bending their backs
Under grim loads. You were an open grave
For gold and love. Always you were the slave
Of crooked thoughts (tortured upon the racks
Of mean mistrust). I made myself as wax
To your fierce seal. I clutched an ebbing wave.

Fool that I was, I loved you ; your harsh soul
Was sweet to me : I gave you with both hands
Love, service, honour, loyalty and praise ;
I would have died for you ! And like a mole
You grubbed and burrowed till the shifting sands
Opened and swallowed up the dream-forged days.

Lighten our Darkness

England, 1918.

In the high places lo ! there is no light,
The ugly dawn beats up forlorn and grey.
Dear Lord, but once before I pass away
Out of this Hell into the starry night
Where still my hopes are set in Death's despite,
Let one great man be good, let one pure ray
Shine through the gloom of this my earthly day
From one tall candle set upon a height.

Judges and prelates, chancellors and kings,
All have I known and suffered and endured,
(And some are quick and some are in their graves).
I looked behind their masks and posturings
And saw their souls too rotten to be cured,
And knew them all for liars, rogues and knaves.

English Benedictines

Chaste poverty, obedience, cloistered peace
And all the trappings of pure holiness,
Faces that smile and hands stretched out to bless,
From Prime to Compline prayers that never cease,
And (flock of lambs with penance whitened fleece)
Troops of fresh boys who pray and sing no less
Devoutly than young angels ; these express
Your conquered flesh and sanctity's increase.

But one child's soul bartered for worldly ease
While Judas fingers pointed the broad road,
One heart bereft, one house made desolate—
Abbot, I tell you, trifles such as these,
Now light as air, shall be a fearful load
When with your monks you stand at heaven's locked gate.

Shelley's Folly, 1919.

On a Showing of the Nativity

See where she lies pale and serene and mild.
Our little Virgin meek and innocent,
The wistful oval of her face down-bent
Upon the wonder of her new-born child.
How frail the stable seems, how fierce and wild
(Outside the intangible angel circle) blent
In fearful hordes the infernal armament,
The dark battalions of the unreconciled!

I saw the vision of our House of Bread,
In liquid fire it floated on the air,
In the blue deeps of night its shining trail
Was suddenly in milky radiance shed,
Against the hope which God hath planted there
Even the gates of Hell shall not prevail.

Before a Crucifix

What hurts Thee most ? The rods ? the thorns ? the nails ?
The crooked wounds that jag Thy bleeding knees ?
(Can ever plummet sound such mysteries ?)
It is perchance the thirst that most prevails
Against Thy stricken flesh, Thy spirit quails
Most at the gall-soaked sponge, the bitter seas
O'erflow with this ? " *Nay, it is none of these.*"
Lord, Lord, reveal it then ere mercy fails.

Is it Thy Mother's anguish ? " *Search thine heart.*
Didst thou not pray to taste the worst with Me,
O thou of little faith." Incarnate Word,
Lord of my soul, I know, it is the part
That Judas played ; this have I shared with Thee
(By wife, child, friend betrayed). " *Thy prayer was heard.*"

Note

GOOD poetry is made up of two things : style and sincerity. Both are requisite in equal degrees. As against this proposition we have two main heresies which, roughly speaking, take in all the bad poetry which is being constantly held up to our admiration by our self-styled critics in *The Morning Post* and elsewhere. There is the " Art for Art's sake " heresy, which upholds style at the expense of sincerity, and there is what I shall denominate the anti-formal heresy, which because its exponents cannot acquire or will not take the trouble to acquire the technique of poetry, claims that strict forms and rules in poetry are inimical to it and may and should be broken whenever it suits the " poet " to break them. The real poet repels both these heresies with equal force.

The average alleged poet of to-day wobbles from one heresy to the other. Occasionally and by accident he may stumble into writing a good poem and this accounts for the rare oasis of poetry which occasionally rewards the weary traveller through the arid desert of rhymed or unrhymed verse which spreads its dismal expanse all round us.

Nowadays we have the phenomenon of an enormous quantity of bad poets writing interminable reams of indifferent verse. There is not a good poet among the lot, but from time to time one or other of them writes a good poem by accident.

The result is that never before in the history of English literature has poetry sunk so low. When a nation which has produced Shakespeare and Marlowe and Chaucer and Milton and Shelley and Wordsworth and Byron and Keats and Tennyson and Blake can seriously lash itself into enthusiasm over the puerile crudities (when they are nothing worse) of a Rupert Brooke, it simply means that poetry is despised and dishonoured and that sane criticism is dead or moribund.

The anti-formal heresy can be briefly dismissed. Carried to its logical conclusion it denies the difference between poetry and prose. Its most extreme exponent was Walt Whitman, who wrote ejaculatory prose and chose to call it poetry. Walt Whitman has been faithfully dealt with by Swinburne, the last of the great poets in the succession of poets, so I need not waste space over him.

The average " poet " who is infected with the anti-formal heresy does not carry it so far as Whitman. He is content to write decasyllabic lines with an occasional eleven-syllabled line or an Alexandrine thrown in between them, and when remonstrated with he will say that he has done it on purpose to produce a certain effect, as who should say " I always play a few false notes in a Chopin concerto, I do it on purpose to produce a certain effect." Or he will write a " sonnet " and break all the rules or some of them and will tell you that he did it on purpose and because he " prefers it that way," the real truth being probably that either he did not know any better, or was gravelled for a rhyme, or is afflicted with a faulty ear for rhythm. The " Irish " school of poetry, with Mr. Yeats at its head, is particularly infected with the anti-formal heresy.

As to the Art for Art's sake heresy, its chief exponent was Oscar Wilde ; and the school of Wilde and his imitators and admirers, rampantly in the ascendant to-day among our " poets " and their " critics," may safely be said to hold the field ; though it is an undoubted fact that many of the victims of Wilde's fallacies in the literary line are quite unconscious of the source of their own convictions concerning the now generally accepted axioms of their art. Wilde's literary gospel can be summed up by saying that he preached all through his writings that in all art style is of more importance than sincerity, and this theory is simply another way of expressing the Art for Art's sake heresy.

Style is the technique of the art of writing, the form into which the artist moulds his ideas. Two persons may have exactly the same idea, and the words by which they respectively express that idea will necessarily fall into the mould of their style. To take a concrete example, the idea expressed by Wordsworth in the first three lines of his " Sonnet on Westminster Bridge," baldly expressed in prose might be represented as follows :

" It is impossible to conceive any earthly scene which would be more beautiful than this ; a man who could fail to be impressed by such a majestic spectacle would indeed be dull and soulless." This is how Wordsworth puts the same idea :

> Earth hath not anything to show more fair,
> Dull would he be of soul who could pass by
> A sight so touching in its majesty. . . .

He takes the idea which might occur to any ordinary man passing over Westminster Bridge on a fresh and beautiful morning, and transmutes it by the alchemy of his style into pure gold. Quite evidently and indisputably then if one wishes to write finely either in prose or poetry, style is of the utmost importance ; but after all that is no more than to say that it takes a poet to write poetry. However sincere a man might be in feeling the beauty of the morning on Westminster Bridge, he could not turn his feeling into poetry unless he had mastered the technique of poetry ; and surely it is equally certain that unless he sincerely felt the beauty, it would never even occur to him to write a poem about it at all. Further, unless a man is so sincere in his feelings of admiration for beauty as to live for a great part of his life under the impulse of such feelings, he would not and could not take the necessary pains to acquire such a difficult art as the art of poetry. When we say that a poet is " born, not made," we simply mean that certain persons have a natural deep instinct about beauty not possessed by other people, which urges them with an irresistible impulse to strive to express what they feel by means of an extraordinarily difficult and complicated art which can only be acquired by taking an enormous amount of trouble. Nobody, I imagine, really believes that a poet is " born " in the sense that he suddenly finds himself in early youth fully equipped with all the power to express himself in flawless verse without taking any trouble about it.

The poet, therefore, is one who puts into a beautiful form the expression of an overpowering emotion, and it follows that his emotion must be quite exceptionally deep and sincere, and that it is the motive power of his style which without the emotion to inspire it would be as useless and dumb as an unplayed violin. To write poetry without sincerity is merely to play with words.

But poetry is an affair of the spirit and people who imagine that they are going to turn themselves into great poets by an inordinate admiration of beautiful material things or beautiful people are fostering the most puerile of delusions. It follows that when I talk of the preoccupation with beauty as being absolutely necessary to the poet, I mean spiritual beauty and nothing else.

The reason of this is that ethical beauty is at the back of all beauty. Beautiful forms, beautiful sounds, beautiful colours, beautiful faces are simply the channels by which spiritual perfection is suggested to our spirit, and the resulting yearning, the desperate struggle upwards of the soul towards the Supreme Beauty, however dimly and darkly felt, is what produces all great art whether in poetry or in music, or in sculpture, or in painting.

That is why all really great Art is founded on and springs from morality. Beauty in the sphere of the spirit is simply goodness in a greater or less degree. The difference between the highest Art and " Art for Art's sake " corresponds to the difference between Philosophy and Sophistry.

Having thus defined my conception of Poetry and the Poet and having indicated what I take to be the two main heresies against which they are essentially opposed, I shall not, in the limited space at my disposal, attempt to follow those heresies into all their ramifications. To do justice to the subject would require a fairly lengthy book. I shall confine myself to making a few remarks about the sonnet because it has always been my favourite instrument of expression in poetry and because I may safely say that no other English poet with the exception of Rossetti (a master of form but to my mind distinctly infected with the " Art for Art's sake " heresy) has devoted so much laborious work to it. Incidentally in passing I will quote my own words and postulate that poets, except in penny novelettes, do not pour out words like inspired gramophones. All good poetry is written slowly and cautiously, with great effort and " unspeakable groanings " of the spirit. It is forged slowly and painfully, and link by link with sweat and blood and tears. The writing of a great poem leaves a poet exhausted. Persons who " pour out words " are rhetoricians and not poets at all.

A recent writer on the English sonnet has taken as the main thesis of a valuable and, in spite of blunders and blemishes, a stimulating book the theory that " the sonnet is the cornerstone of English poetry," and that " all the finest poets have been either fine sonneteers or unconscious workers in the sonnet movement " and that " there is no poetry of the highest that does not in some sort distinguishably ally itself with sonnet poetry." I dissent altogether from these propositions. I think they are fantastic and not in any way borne out by the facts. So far from the sonnet being the corner-stone of English poetry, it would, I think, be very easy to prove that it has always been a somewhat forlorn exotic and that very few of the great English poets have thoroughly understood it. However, as the author of the book to which I am referring has made his theory the vehicle for a fine and spirited appreciation of poetry and the sonnet, and as his theory does not involve any fundamental heresy, I shall not here further join issue with him, having said what I had to say on the matter in another place. It is otherwise when I come to consider the attack which he has made on the rhyming of words ending with the ē or ee sound and words ending in " y." Such an attack is dangerous to poetry, and unless it is answered, in view of the fact that the writer of the book speaks with a certain amount of authority and is himself (though tainted with the anti-formal heresy) a not inconsiderable poet, it might have a very disastrous effect on those aspiring youths who may take him as an infallible guide. I am the more concerned to answer him inasmuch as he has done me the honour of taking fourteen rhymes of my own out of my " Sonnets " published in 1909 and putting them in a pillory as examples of careless rhyming. It is to be remarked that he does not mention my name, and in discussing his charge against me I am returning the compliment—if it be a compliment. I now quote what he says.

" A collection of nineteen otherwise excellent sonnets published recently has the following rhymes : me, memory, colloquy, thee ; hostility, me, knee, hypocrisy ; Italy,

122

memory, be, minstrelsy ; loyalty, me ; ecstasy, eternity ; grudgingly, immortality ; thee, symmetry, sea, immortality ; curiosity, thee, tree, flee ; inconstancy, thee. Thus is poetical indolence justified of her children, and thus is the writing of sonnets reduced to a species of Kindergarten entertainment. Of course we must still love and be thankful for these easy and inspired purveyors of easy and uninspired rhyming ; but how much more closely we could have loved them, and how much more thankful could we have been for them, if they had toiled a little as well as spun."

I cannot do better in reply to this somewhat spiteful onslaught than to reproduce the appended extracts from a letter which I sent the gentleman in question as soon as I noticed the passage above quoted from his book.

SHELLEY'S FOLLY,
LEWES,
Feb. 25, 1918.

DEAR ——

Cast your eye over the following rhymes taken from Shakespeare's sonnets : die, memory. husbandry, posterity. legacy, free. usury, thee. thee, posterity. (these last two in the same sonnet). Eye, majesty. astronomy, quality. sky, memory. eye, alchemy. poverty, injury. thee, melancholy. eye, gravity. dye, wantonly. eternity,* posterity.* liberty, injury. pry, jealousy. eye, remedy. antiquity,* iniquity.* (last two in same sonnet). fortify, memory. cry, jollity. authority,* simplicity. (last two in same sonnet). Impiety,* society.* memory, eternity. fly, majesty. eye, history. die, dignity. idolatry, be. prophecies, eyes. flattery, alchemy. tyranny, incertainty. canopy, eternity. lies, subtilties. constancy,* see.* by, remedy.

I have left out the *innumerable* rhymes of " thee " " me," " be," " sea," etc.   The rhymes I have marked with an * are bad rhymes because there is the same consonant sound in them.   Nowhere in my sonnets have I used such rhymes,† and my rhymes which you " pilloried " in your book (page 260) are, every one of them, correct and, in most cases, beautiful and carefully sought out.   Also, it is to be noted that I have written all my sonnets in the strictest Petrarchan form which makes much greater demands on rhymes than the easy Shakespearian sonnet (which, since it avoids all the technical difficulties, is not really a sonnet at all.)   I have no time to wade through Wordsworth's sonnets, but the two best, quoted in your book, have : by, majesty (a beautiful rhyme), and free, tranquillity (equally good).   In short, what you try to impute to me as a blemish is an ornament. . . .

The truth is, of course, that rhymes of this character belong to the genius of the English language and form one of its greatest beauties.   The frequency with which they have been used by all our greatest poets, without any exception whatever, is accounted for partly by their beauty and partly by the great quantity of words in our language which end with the ē and y sounds.

In conclusion, I should like to point out that what I and the author of the book I have referred to call " the strict Petrarchan form " of the sonnet, is, in my opinion, the best and the most beautiful.   Personally I have never used any other and I was using it at least fifteen years before the gentleman in question had either written a sonnet himself or set up as an authority on the subject.   At the same time

† This statement is not quite correct.   In some of my earlier Sonnets I have been occasionally guilty of this lapse.

it must be observed that there is no real authority for calling it the best form. The author of the book I have referred to is, apparently, not aware that Petrarch was not the inventor of the sonnet in Italy and that even he (Petrarch) himself occasionally has a rhymed couplet at the end of his sestets. A little knowledge is a dangerous thing.

As regards my own poems which are now collected together in this volume, I should like to say that they comprise work scattered over a period of nearly thirty years. For the childish egoism and the dubious morality of such pieces as " Apologia " and " Ode to my Soul," and one or two of the earlier sonnets I hold no kind of brief, but at the same time I have felt that while I might be justified in altering and revising faults of technique, it would be foolish to change the essential character of pieces which are representative of various stages of my development as a man and as a poet. Accordingly I have left them exactly as they were written.

Certain other poems of mine which appeared in an edition published in Paris in 1896, with a French translation, I have refrained from putting into this collected edition for the same reason which caused me to refuse to include them in " The City of the Soul," published in 1899 (third edition published 1911) and which impelled me to withhold permission for the republication of the entire Paris edition which has been more than once urged on me by the *Mercure de France*, who were my first publishers. I am well aware that having written these poems I cannot escape responsibility for them, and I have no kind of doubt that after my death they will eventually be reprinted. My reason for omitting them from this edition is that, although there is no actual harm in them, they lend themselves to evil interpretations, and the fact that they have so been interpreted by those whose interest it has been to attack and defame me and that they have actually been used against me in the law courts by the very persons who most applauded them at the time they were written, has given me a distaste for them which such poetical merits as they may possess are insufficient to dispel.

ALFRED BRUCE DOUGLAS.

SHELLEY'S FOLLY, LEWES,
February, 1919.